TRADITIONAL MUSLIM NETWORKS: PAKISTAN'S UNTAPPED RESOURCE IN THE FIGHT AGAINST TERRORISM

A Report of the WORDE Initiative, "Understanding the Socio-Political Dynamics of Pakistan"

By Hedieh Mirahmadi, Mehreen Farooq, and Waleed Ziad
May 2010

ABOUT WORDE

WORDE IS A NONPROFIT, EDUCATIONAL ORGANIZATION whose mission is to enhance communication and understanding between Muslim and non-Muslim communities and to strengthen moderate Muslim institutions worldwide to mitigate social and political conflict.

Our work is guided by the belief that terrorism is bred by ignorance and is fanned by extremists who attempt to legitimize political agendas by framing their rhetoric in religious terminology. With the right resources and education, moderate religious leaders and their institutions can serve as a prime bulwark against radicalism.

WORDE shapes public policy by cultivating a better understanding of Islamic tenets that promote pluralism and service to humanity -- while exposing the roots of extremism that disrupt the peaceful coexistence of Muslims and non-Muslims everywhere. Our specialists are academics, theologians, development experts, and policy analysts who design effective, long-term solutions in the key areas of educational reform, resource development, and international security.

ACKNOWLEDGEMENTS

OUR HEARTFELT GRATITUDE GOES OUT TO the esteemed delegates of this project who risk their lives every day, and have each suffered personal tragedy, to save the civilized world from terrorism and radical Islamism. We hope that we have done justice to their story and have brought new insights about the gravity of this international threat. We are also thankful to Zeyno Baran at the Hudson Institute; Peter Bergen and the staff at the New America Foundation; Congresswoman Sue Myrick and her staff; Ziad Alahdad, former Director of Operations of the World Bank; Mateen Siddiqui, VP of ISCA; Faryal Naveed for her graphic design and printing talents; as well as the various US government agencies who hosted the delegates during their visit.

CONTENTS

Executive Summary	1
Introduction	4
Pakistan's Ideological Divide	5
History of Deobandi-Wahhabi Encroachment	10
Talibanization of Pakistan's Frontier	16
The Militant's Campaign against Traditional Islam	18
Public Opinion in Pakistan	20
Recommendations	21
The Impact of Courting the 'Soft Taliban'	25
Conclusion	27

EXECUTIVE SUMMARY

IN APRIL 2010, WORDE HOSTED A HIGH LEVEL PAKISTANI DELEGATION, which included a current Federal Minister, and convened a weeklong series of meetings with US policymakers in Washington DC. The delegates represent Pakistan's traditional, moderate Muslim majority, popularly known as the ASJ [an acronym for *Ahl as-Sunnah wa'l-Jama'ah*[1]]. The ASJ leadership, who are amongst the country's most respected leaders and primary providers of education and social services, have spearheaded national campaigns against extremism. The delegates met with officials at the US Departments of State, Defense, and USAID, as well as with lawmakers on Capitol Hill, think tanks, community groups and NGOs to provide practical insights into the culture, history and hierarchy of sociopolitical groups in Pakistan. The delegates explained how vast regions of the Khyber-Pakhtunkhwa province (formally the North West Frontier Province, or NWFP) and the Federally Administered Tribal Areas (FATA) are now overrun with extremists, and how their growing influence runs contrary to centuries of traditional culture in the area. These experts described the process by which whole traditional communities have been uprooted, leaving behind a safe haven for the radical Taliban and Al-Qaeda elements. In their remarks, the delegates provided concrete solutions to the problem and gave predictions on future success if those recommendations were implemented.

The program was an opportunity to learn how radical groups operate, how anti-*jihadist* forces in Pakistan view the current political climate, and how they believe the ultimate battle for Pakistan's future will be won.
WORDE has outlined four broad policy recommendations that developed as a result of the recent visit:

- In parallel with military efforts against extremist groups in Pakistan, there needs to be a long term strategy of empowering moderate Muslim networks

---

[1]. *Ahl as-Sunnah wa'l-Jama'ah* literally translates as "People of the tradition of the Prophet and the community" and includes those commonly referred to as *Barelvi*.

Executive Summary

who share our common goals of preserving the Pakistani state and encouraging the common values of human liberty, freedom of expression and social harmony. In this regard, the US must recognize the important role of traditional ASJ religious leaders, and create partnerships with their institutions and networks which impact millions of people in Pakistan. This will serve to strengthen the moderate voice and broaden their legitimacy, both at the local and international levels.

- Second, the international donor community should help bolster the position of moderate religious leaders vis-à-vis extremist ideologues by providing financial assistance to a wide range of their activities For example, the ASJ leaders need to strengthen the institutional capacity of their social welfare, educational, and political organizations; they need leadership training for their progressive political parties and media outreach; they would like communications and public relations training to strengthen the moderate voice; and they seek organizational support for conferences that promote unity and peace, as well as other educational programs that condemn terrorism and religious radicalism.

- Third, the US should demonstrate American goodwill by working within established networks of the moderate religious leadership to administer aid, carry out development projects, and provide rapid-response humanitarian assistance. By establishing partnerships to provide social services and educational institutions to improve the lives of the Pakistani people, the US can help strengthen moderate institutions, and delegitimize *jihadist* networks who build their support base by providing social services to those most in need.

- In furtherance of the counterinsurgency [COIN] objectives in Pakistan and the need for "reintegration and reconciliation" of extremists who are not driven solely by radical ideology, these traditional ASJ leaders and clerics have the local legitimacy to peel away the terrorist recruits who enlist with the Taliban due to dire circumstances – unemployment, abject poverty, or political grievances. COIN tools should not be limited only to engaging with the central government, which can be slow to provide social services in conflict-affected areas, and which often lacks credibility at the local level because of historical political and social grievances. The COIN strategy should include utilizing the existing ASJ civil society infrastructure as part of the "hold and build" mechanism particularly in post-conflict zones, which would guarantee long term sustainability and buy-in of the local populations.

INTRODUCTION

PAKISTAN, AN IMPORTANT SOUTH ASIA REGIONAL ALLY OF THE US, is home to approximately 175 million Muslims, the vast majority of which practice moderate traditional Islam and reject Al-Qaeda/Taliban's brand of religion.

To effectively counter the rise of religious extremism or *"Talibanism"* as it is often referred to, the international community needs to establish relationships with moderate traditional and cultural leaders in Pakistan. The network of traditional mainstream Muslims known as the ASJ [an acronym for *Ahl as-Sunnah wa'l-Jama'ah*[1]] are amongst the most respected community leaders, clerics and activists who wield considerable influence even in the troubled frontier which is otherwise inaccessible to outsiders. For decades, they have been primary providers of social services and education throughout the country and are a vital resource for mobilizing the population at the grassroots level.

The challenge is recognizing which religious leaders to work with, and how their institutions can help in countering *Talibanization*. US policy makers must be able to distinguish *jihadist* fighters from traditional Muslim leaders who are our natural allies on the ground, but who find themselves continually sidelined by efforts to court the extremists into negotiations. Alienating this major force at the grassroots level serves as a dangerous recruiting tool because it engenders further mistrust amongst the local population and provides "negative incentives" for recruits to join extremist's causes. Therefore, understanding the ideological divide in Pakistan is critically important to developing both effective military strategies and economic development programs.

---

1. *Ahl as-Sunnah wa'l-Jama'ah* literally translates as "People of the tradition of the Prophet and the community."

PAKISTAN'S IDEOLOGICAL DIVIDE

RELIGIOUS LEADERS OF ALL DENOMINATIONS WIELD considerable power and influence as some of the primary educators and social services providers in Pakistan. They are amongst the most trusted leaders, often serving on *jirgas* in tribal areas, and playing an integral role as counselors and mediators of conflict. Their institutions – from mosques, schools, soup kitchens, and health services facilities at the local level, to political parties and media outlets at the national level – lie at the core of Pakistan's society. In order to wage a successful counterinsurgency strategy, the Pakistan central government *and* the international community, needs to establish a good working relationship with the traditional religious and cultural leadership.

A prerequisite to determining whom to work with is to avoid treating all religious elements as one monolith. There is a vast difference between the *Deobandi-Wahhabi* (DW) religious networks which mushroomed during the Soviet invasion of Afghanistan, and the ASJ, who are the indigenous religious leaders, espousing peaceful mainstream Islamic practices.

AHL AS-SUNNAH WA'L-JAMA'AH (ASJ)-PAKISTAN'S MODERATE MAJORITY

ASJ and its various organizational groups represent the mainstream form of Islam most practiced in Pakistan and includes the practitioners commonly referred to as the *Barelvis*. ASJ Muslims – which form the majority even in the tribal frontier regions – practice a combination of the classical Sunni-Hanafi school of thought and the mystical teachings of Sufism. These teachings embody concepts of moderation, good moral character, and social cohesion, which have facilitated the peaceful coexistence of Muslims and non-Muslims in South Asia for centuries.

SCOPE AND IMPACT OF ASJ INSTITUTIONS

ASJ leadership and their institutions are active at all levels of Pakistani society. They are members of the National Assembly and Provincial Assemblies, and have founded political parties including the Pakistan Awami Tehreek which aims to improve the state of human rights, justice and women's rights in Pakistan, as well as the Nizam-e-Mustafa Party.[2] In May 2009, eight political parties of the ASJ came together under the banner of the Sunni Ittehad Council (SIC) to take a stand against *Talibanization* and in support of Pakistan's military operations in Swat and Waziristan.[3] Though some of the ASJ parties may be socially conservative, they doctrinally reject the violent, expansionist goals of the DW factions.

The ASJ have established thousands of educational institutions across the country with religious as well as secular curricula, and play a major role in providing and promoting female education in Pakistan. For example, the ASJ Jamia Anwar-ul-Uloom Multan, one of the leading educational centers of Pakistan, and its sister school the Jamia L'il-Banaat for women, oversee a network of 150 schools.[4] The Jamia Anwar-ul-Uloom women's schools provide education, clothing and shelter for 15,000 women. Another leading ASJ educational organization is Minhaj-ul-Quran International with offices, educational and community centers in more than 80 countries.[5] In total Minhaj-ul-Quran manages approximately 1000 educational institutes, including libraries in Pakistan and a university based in Lahore. The Dawat-e-Islami network has over 300 moderate *madrasas*[6] in Karachi, and under its Madrasa-t'ul-Madina network, 42,000 students are educated free of charge. The network of moderate ASJ *madrasas* across the country are centrally registered under the Tanzeem-ul-Madaris Ahl-e-Sunnat ASJ education board.

ASJ educators are actively promoting education in conflict and post-conflict areas. For example, one organization of ASJ leaders in the Khyber Agency in FATA has recently built a network of 90 schools in the Agency, particularly schools for women, providing education for over 7,000 students. ASJ leaders in FATA are

---

2. Pakistani Awami Tehrik: Putting People First, http://www.pat.com.pk.
3. Nisar Mehdi, "SIC supports Waziristan operation," *The Nation*, November 02, 2009.
4. Tarikh Jami'a Anwar-ul-Uloom Multan, http://www.kazmis.com/tanwar.html.
5. Minhaj-ul-Quran International, http://www.minhaj.org/english/index.html.
6. *Madrasa* is an Islamic religious school. Although the Arabic and Urdu plural of the word is *madaris*, the plural utilized is the conventional English form.

making efforts to replace the over 200 schools – mostly girls' schools - that have been demolished by extremists.

There are also a number of prominent ASJ student organizations, notably the Anjuman Talaba-e-Islam (ATI). ATI is one of Pakistan's largest student organizations, with 800 branches across the country. ATI members have organized numerous rallies against extremism, and the organization places a major emphasis on social welfare and improvement of the educational sector.[7]

Additionally, ASJ institutions are some of the primary providers of social services, with charitable and welfare organizations countrywide.[8] Notably, the ASJ Al-Mustafa Welfare Trust is the second largest social services provider in Pakistan, providing health services, aid for the destitute, widows, orphans, and handicapped, as well as orphanages and free schooling. Al-Mustafa Welfare Trust was a major provider of humanitarian assistance to victims of the 2005 Kashmir earthquake, and recently has embarked on a campaign to eradicate polio in partnership with the World Health Organization (WHO), UNICEF, and Rotary International.[9] Another prominent organization is the Junaidi Foundation, one of the major social services providers in FATA.

ASJ mosques and shrines across Pakistan serve as forums for some of the largest cultural events in the country, and serve as focal points for local communities. Regular celebrations of the Prophet Muhammad's birthday (known as *Mawlid* celebrations) and of traditional saints (known as *Urs* celebrations), occur throughout the year, drawing hundreds of thousands of people. These celebrations are attended by Muslims and non-Muslims alike, and men and women from all walks of life. Emphasizing social cohesion and denouncing religious radicalism at such events, ASJ leaders are able to mobilize the masses of Pakistan's society which abhors extremism and resent the association of Islam with the brutality of the militants.[10]

---

7. Delegate comments during recent visit to Washington DC in April, 2010.
8. Ibid.
9. Aziz Memon and Haji Muhammad Hanif Tayyab, *Ulema Convention: Role of Ulema in Polio Eradication*. (Rotary International Pakistan, 2010).
10. "Of Saints and Sinners," *Economist*, December 18, 2008.

ASJ scholars and activists hold regular conferences and congregations across the country. For example, the ASJ umbrella organization Jamaat-e-Ahl-e-Sunnat organizes regular nationwide conferences, while Dawat-e-Islami's annual congregation in Multan is reputed to be the largest annual congregation after the Islamic pilgrimage to Mecca.

ASJ institutions disseminate their message of moderation through the publication and distribution of books, educational pamphlets, and electronic media. ASJ institutions also host TV channels, such as the 24 hour Madani Channel. Many ASJ programs build bridges between different ethnic, social, and religious groups. This has positioned ASJ leaders at the forefront of interfaith work, and in efforts towards ending sectarian violence.[11]

ASJ in the Forefront of the Struggle against Religious Extremism

Given their practice of classical traditional Islam, ASJ leaders share a mutual interest with US policymakers in eliminating the radical Islamist threat. Amongst the most active in countering terrorism, these moderate religious leaders have organized a large social movement against the Taliban. In the past year as the number of terrorist attacks increased in Pakistan, ASJ leaders have doubled their efforts, particularly in war-affected areas. As one ASJ leader described, "at the time when people were afraid to speak out against terrorism out of fear for their lives, we spoke out because it is our religious duty."

From the "Save Pakistan Convention" in June 2009 to the "Ulema Convention" in December 2009, ASJ leaders launched numerous campaigns and conferences to galvanize the population and forge unity amongst the various religious schools of thought against the Taliban.[12] Recently, to counter Taliban propaganda condemning polio vaccinations as a Western conspiracy aimed to sterilize the population, the Al-Mustafa Welfare Trust, in conjunction with moderate religious

---

11. Delegate comments during recent visit to Washington DC in April, 2010.
12. Tahaffuz-e-Pakistan Ulema-o-Mashaykh Convention, Minhaj ul-Quran Internatinoal, http://www.minhaj.org/english/tid/8462/Tahaffuz-e-Pakistan-Ulema-o-Mashaykh-Convention.html.

leaders and medical experts, organized conferences throughout Pakistan exposing this dangerous myth.[13]

ASJ leaders have also issued several key religious rulings against extremism. Last year, the Sunni Ittehad Council alliance of moderate religious parties led a country-wide movement to issue religious rulings denouncing the Taliban.[14] More recently, in January 2010, Dr. Tahir ul-Qadri, the director of Minhaj-ul-Quran, issued a 600 page *fatwa* (ruling) denouncing suicide bombings and terrorism, declaring them un-Islamic.[15] Such rulings issued by prominent ASJ leaders serve to delegitimize the Taliban's extremist ideology at the popular level.

Deobandi-Wahabism (DW)

In contrast to the teachings of ASJ, many of the DW groups advocate a puritanical, often militant, form of Islam. Their common aim is to create a new Islamic empire that is ruled according to their own narrow interpretation of the Muslim faith. Hard-line DW groups adhere to the doctrine of *takfir*, whereby all Muslims of different persuasions are categorized as apostates and may be legitimately targeted and executed. Although DW Muslims are a minority in Pakistan, their ideology has given rise to menacing political movements including al-Qaeda, the Taliban, and dozens of militant outfits and political parties.

Militant DW groups have launched a systematic campaign to undermine the identity of Pakistan's moderate majority by targeting and killing moderate religious leaders and those who question their ideology. According to the former Federal Minister Hanif Tayyab, "In the Frontier, the militant organizations have terrorized every walk of life. They murder, steal, and kidnap, all in the name of religion. The terrorism that has engulfed NWFP has affected the ASJ community the most."[16]

---

13. Aziz Memon and Haji Muhammad Hanif Tayyab, *Ulema Convention: Role of Ulema in Polio Eradication*.
14. Delegate comments during recent visit to Washington DC in April 2010.
15. Dominic Casciani, "Islamic Scholar Tahir ul-Qadri Issues Terrorism Fatwa," *BBC News*, March 2, 2010, http://news.bbc.co.uk/2/hi/uk_news/8544531.stm (accessed May 3, 2010).
16. Hanif Tayyab, personal interview, May, 2010.

HISTORY OF DEOBANDI–WAHHABI ENCROACHMENT

In addition to their militant outfits, the DW have built an elaborate system of organizations and institutions that work together to undermine traditional Islam and fill the ranks for their international extremist networks. Their success is evident in the growing radicalization of Pakistani society since the early 1980s. THE THEOLOGICAL ONSLAUGHT OF THE EXTREMIST SECTS did not permeate Pakistan until the US, Saudi Arabia, and the Pakistani central government used radical Islamists as a bulwark against the Russians during the Russo-Afghan war. That policy meant that heavy weapons and vast financial resources were concentrated in the hands of DW leaders whose practice of Islam was radically different from the majority of the indigenous population. After the defeat of Soviet forces in Afghanistan in 1989, the DW groups have continued to use these resources throughout Pakistan to exert their control over religious, social and political life. The majority of their work is carried out primarily under the auspices of two principal political organizations: the Deobandi *Jamiat Ulema-i-Islam* (JUI) and the Wahhabi-inspired *Jamaat-e-Islami* (JI).

The JI was founded in India in 1940 by Sayyid Abul A'la Maududi (1903-1979 CE), a radical revolutionary who was greatly influenced by the Muslim Brotherhood movement. With the partition of India in 1947, Maududi shifted the JI's headquarters to the newly formed Pakistan, though it still maintains branches in both India and Bangladesh.[17]

Until March 2009, the JI was led by Qazi Hussain Ahmad, a firebrand who was placed under house arrest on November 3, 2001, for inciting anti-American demonstrations in Pakistan.[18] Ahmad has called for an end to cooperation between the US and Pakistan,[19] denouncing it "an alliance against the country and the

---

17. Founder of Jamaat e- Islami, Jamaat-e-Islami, http://jamaat.org/beta/site/page/3.
18. "Qazi Hussain Ahmad Released," *Jamaat-e-Islami Pakistan Press Release*, February 28, 2002.
19. Nisar Mehdi "US Creating Anarchy in Pakistan: Qazi," *The Nation*, October 17, 2008, http://www.nation.com.pk/pakistan-news-newspaper-daily-english-online/Regional/Karachi/17-Oct-2008/US-creating-anarchy-in-Pakistan-Qazi (accessed April 17, 2010).

ummah [Muslim nation]." The current leader, Syed Munawar Hasan, has vehemently opposed military operations against the Taliban.[20]

Most of the JI's leaders are political elites with secular educational backgrounds. In contrast, most of the JUI's leaders are clerics.

The JUI is the political arm of the Deobandi movement, a highly conservative religious movement associated with a vast network of *madrasas*. Deoband traces its origins to the Dar-ul-Uloom founded in the town of Deoband, India, in 1867.

Particularly after the Soviet Union invaded Afghanistan in 1979, many Deobandi *madrasas* in Pakistan's tribal areas were converted into militant training camps for *mujahidin*, and Deobandi JUI leaders turned their attention towards militancy and *jihad* in Afghanistan, as well as in Kashmir and other parts of the world. Today, their list of enemies has expanded to include the United States, the United Nations and the West in general.[21]

Like the Wahhabi-inspired JI, the Deobandi JUI advocate a militant, puritanical form of Islam. Though ostensibly religious, both groups share a focus that is primarily political. Just as the Wahhabis have given birth to al-Qaeda, the Deobandi JUI movement was the primary theological influence on Afghanistan's Taliban.[22]

In April 2001, the JUI hosted a world Deobandi conference in Peshawar. Leaders of the JI also attended the event. During the conclave, JUI leaders credited their Deobandi movement with inspiring the Taliban.[23] Indeed, one of the keynote addresses at the event was delivered – via tape – by the Taliban's supreme leader, Mullah Omar. Other speakers included Osama Bin Laden, whose speech was prerecorded.[24]

The JUI's leader, Fazlur Rehman, also spoke at the Peshawar conference. He warned the West to stop its "aggression against the Muslims or face the

---

20. "JI Chief Calls for Talks with Taliban," *Dawn*, May 15, 2010, http://www.dawn.com/wps/wcm/connect/dawn-content-library/dawn/the-newspaper/local/lahore/ji-chief-calls-for-talks-with-taliban-550 (accessed May 15, 2010).
21. *Deobandi Islam: The Religion of the Taliban*, United States Navy, Chaplain Corps.
22. Arif Jamal, "The Growth of the Deobandi Jihad in Afghanistan," *The Jamestown Foundation Terrorism Monitor*, 8:2, January 14, 2010.
23. Rahimullah Yusufzai, "Muslims Suffering Due to West's Conspiracies," *The News International, Pakistan*, April 10, 2001.
24. United States Navy, Chaplain Corps, *Deobandi Islam*.

consequences."[25] Rehman continues to call for the formation of an Islamic state in Pakistan similar to the one created by the Taliban in Afghanistan.[26] One delegate explained that just recently in a session in Parliament, Fazlur Rehman stood up in defense of the Taliban in Pakistan and when questioned about it later, admitted he did it to garner US interests as an "interlocutor" of the Taliban.[27]

Another prominent JUI leader is Sami ul-Haq, a Pakistani senator and cleric that has often been seen with Bin Laden. He operates the largest of the militant JUI *madrasas* in Pakistan's Khyber-Pakhtunkhwa province, the *Haqqanya*, a school whose alumni include the "American Taliban," John Walker Lindh, as well as most of the senior leaders of the Taliban movement itself.[28]

Although the Deobandi JUI and the Wahhabi-inspired JI disagree on some theological matters, they have nonetheless forged a powerful political alliance, the impact of which is felt well beyond Pakistan's borders.

The JUI and the JI regularly field candidates in local and national elections, though neither party has secured enough seats in either the Senate or the National Assembly to exercise any real influence on Pakistani politics. However, they do make their influence felt in other ways. Both organizations operate largely within the legal political framework, but they both also allegedly sponsor and support a number of illegal terrorist organizations.[29]

JI allegedly has had direct ties to armed groups fighting in Kashmir, such as the *Hizb-ul-Mujahideen*.[30] Like the JUI, it has also provided support to the Taliban in Afghanistan. Other armed Kashmiri groups with alleged links to the JI and JUI include the *Harakat ul-Mujahedeen*, the *Lashkar-e-Taiba* and the *Jaish-e-Muhammad*.[31]

---

25. Anwar Iqbal, "Analysis: Muslim Radicals Flex Muscles," *United Press International*, April 9, 2001.
26. Raja Asghar, "Moral Brigade Wants Indian Films Off Pakistan Cables," *Dawn*, August 12, 2009, http://www.dawn.com/wps/wcm/connect/dawn-content-library/dawn/news/culture/04-moral-brigade-wants-indian-films-off-pakistan-cables-qs-02 (accessed May 18, 2010).
27. Delegate comment during visit to Washington, DC in April, 2010.
28. Imtiaz Ali, "The Father of the Taliban: An Interview with Maulana Sami ul-Haq," *The Jamestown Foundation Spotlight on Terror*, 4:2 , May 23, 2007, http://www.jamestown.org/programs/gta/single/?tx_ttnews%5Btt_news%5D=4180&tx_ttnews%5BbackPid%5D=26&cHash=2feb32fe98 (accessed April 15, 2010)
29. Frederic Grare, "Pakistan: The Myth of an Islamist Peril," *Carnegie Endowment for Peace Policy Brief*, 45, (February, 2006).
30. Jessica Stern, "Pakistan's Jihad Culture," *Foreign Affairs*, (November/December 2000).
31. K. Alan Kronstadt, "International Terrorism in South Asia," CRS Report for Congress, November 3, 2003: 5-6.

These groups also have direct ties to Bin Laden's terrorist network. In 1998, for example, *Harakat* leader Farooq Kashmiri Khalil signed Bin Laden's declaration of war against the United States. Intelligence officials also suspect Bin Laden of providing funding to *Jaish*. The founder of *Jaish*, Masood Azhar, is known to have met with Bin Laden several times in Afghanistan.[32] In addition, the JUI is associated with Pakistan's *Sipah-i-Sahaba*, a terrorist organization that is blamed for the deaths of thousands of Pakistani Shiites over the past decade.[33]

While the JI and the JUI have focused much of their efforts on Kashmir and Afghanistan, both organizations have brought their "holy war" home to Pakistan itself, in an effort to replace the existing secular regime with a religious one. Even more troubling is the fact that both organizations advocate a political and military *jihad* against the West.

DEOBANDI MADRASAS – CENTERS OF RADICALIZATION

There are few countries outside of Saudi Arabia and the Gulf States, where the influence of the transnational DW movement is more pervasive than in Pakistan. In an area where unemployment is high and literacy is low, the Wahhabis have taken the opportunity to invest money from the Gulf States to construct new mosques and schools, creating a system of recruitment and indoctrination that offers young Pakistanis a free education, a chance to travel abroad and the promise of a respectable career.[34]

Once a new DW mosque is complete and staffed, DW teachers begin offering basic Qur'an classes. Most of the students who attend these classes come from financially disadvantaged families. Their parents are often eager to see their children take advantage of such educational opportunities, which, generally speaking, they could not otherwise afford.

When a sufficient number of students have become active in these classes, the mosque is transformed into a *madrasa* in which the curriculum emphasizes hardline DW doctrines. Students that move on into this expanded program generally

---

32. "Terrorism: Questions and Answers," *The Council on Foreign Relations and the Markle Foundation* (2002).
33. Iqbal, "Analysis: Muslim Radicals Flex Muscles."
34. Delegate comment during visit to Washington, DC in April, 2010.

spend six or seven years studying at the *madrasa*. Upon completion, the most promising are offered fellowships abroad to continue their religious education and political indoctrination. There, they study with some of the leading ideologues of the Wahhabi sect. The students who excel in this advanced course of study will return to Pakistan with money to start their own mosques, and begin a new cycle of recruitment and indoctrination. Those that are unable to secure funding are assigned to teach in established *madrasas*. The result is a remarkably efficient and frighteningly effective system for recruiting and radicalizing legions of young militants.[35]

This system bears remarkable similarities with other religious cults. Young recruits are "estranged from their families; forbidden to have any contact with them" according to the Delegation. The movement, they are told, is their new family. The militants tell their young disciples that people living a normal life – who watch television and buy and sell Western products – are the partners of the "unbelievers." This applies to both their parents and the larger Muslim society. Anyone who fails to accept the DW system is considered an enemy of Islam and is to be treated accordingly.

In contrast to the well-funded DW *madrasa* system, moderate ASJ madrasas suffer greatly from a lack of funding and support, especially since the Gulf State resources have gone almost exclusively to the more extreme factions. As one delegate described, "While the DW have grand, beautiful buildings with modern amenities and computers, our schools are small and poorly equipped. We constantly lose students [to DW *madrasas*] because of the stipends [DW *madrasas*] provide to their students. We simply cannot compete without international support to modernize our facilities and provide adequate teacher training."

The Afghan Jihad

Though DW factions had been working to undermine the traditional *madrasa* system in Pakistan for decades, the radicalization of religious schools accelerated rapidly during the 1980s.

---

35. Delegates explain the process of DW recruiting, during discussions with WORDE staff April 2010 in Washington DC.

The transnational DW movement saw the Soviet invasion of Afghanistan as an opportunity to revive the spirit of *jihad* against non-Muslims. To this end, DW factions recruited thousands of young Muslims from around the world to fight there. These recruits were first sent to Pakistan. There, they received military training in special camps along the border with Afghanistan, as well as theological and ideological training in nearby *madrasas*. One of the principal coordinators of this recruitment effort was Osama Bin Laden himself.

"The operation was devised by the Pakistani Inter-Services Intelligence (ISI) and the Saudi Ministry of Intelligence, headed by Prince Turki Bin Faysal, with the approval of the CIA," says Olivier Roy, an expert on Islamic extremism.[36] "Simply put, the idea was to promote an Islamic fundamentalism closer to the Wahhabi school of thought official in Saudi Arabia."

United States intelligence officials believed this was an effective means of building an anti-Communist army. It was also seen as an effective way of destabilizing revolutionary Iran. According to Roy, "Washington conceived a plan to make Moscow pay the maximum price for its occupation of Afghanistan while turning Islamic radicalism against the Communists and, as a spin-off, against Iranian Shiite."[37]

Pakistan hoped to leverage its support for this training program to gain greater influence in Central Asia. For the Saudis, however, it was a means of promoting and expanding the international Wahhabi movement.[38]

The United States had little use for this network of *madrasas* and training camps after the defeat of the Soviet Union in 1989. Funding from Washington was suspended. However, the system continued to function, though its focus shifted. Instead of training militants to do battle against the USSR, new recruits were trained for battle in the Balkans, Kashmir and, ultimately, the United States.

---

36. Olivier Roy, "Changing Patterns among Radical Islamic Movements," *Brown Journal of World Affairs* 6:1 (Winter/Spring 1999).
37. Olivier Roy, "Hazy Outlines of an Islamist International: Fundamentalists without a Common Cause," *Le Monde Diplomatique*, October 4, 1998.
38. "Jihad and the Saudi Petrodollar," BBC News, November 15, 2007.

TALIBANIZATION OF PAKISTAN'S FRONTIER

During the Afghan civil war that followed in 1989, various elements in Pakistan, afraid that the unrest would spill over into Pakistan, supported a group of nearly pure Deobandi-based *jihadist* militias in Afghanistan. These militias assumed power in Afghanistan in 1996 as the Taliban, and increasingly came under the influence of Al-Qaeda and other transnational Wahhabi terrorist groups which sought to export their ideology to other Muslim states. This led to the gradual *Talibanization* of pockets of Pakistan's frontier regions bordering Afghanistan, as these militants traveled back and forth to re-fortify, train, and recruit, especially from the DW *madrasas* in the region.

The Pakistani Taliban, which increasingly controls large swathes of FATA, comprises a number of loosely knit decentralized DW militant and criminal factions. Each faction operates largely under a separate agenda. By 2007 the groups came together under the banner of the Tehrik-i-Taliban Pakistan (TTP).[39] TTP militants have attacked Pakistani state targets, Western targets, and ASJ and Shi'a groups as well. Since 2008 the TTP have initiated a campaign of suicide attacks on Pakistan's major cities. They have been able to expand their influence into other parts of Pakistan with support from long-established DW extremist networks based primarily in the Punjab who have historically targeted ASJ and Shi'a Muslims.[40]

TTP factions tend to be well funded through wealthy individuals in the Persian Gulf, as well as through the drug trade, smuggling, and kidnapping activities. As a result, they provide attractive incentives to lure people into their movement. According to a delegate, a single militant group in the Mohmand Agency in FATA is known to carry out 20 kidnappings a day, earning between 2–20 million rupees per kidnapping.

---

39. Mukhtar Khan, "Pakistan's Most Wanted: A Profile of Tehrik-e-Taliban Leader Baitullah Mahsud," *The Jamestown Foundation Terrorism Monitor*, 7:10, April 24, 2009.
40. Hassan Abbas, "Defining the Punjabi Taliban Network," *CTC Sentinel*, 2:4, April, 2009.

TTP groups have capitalized on poverty and unemployment particularly in FATA, offering generous salaries, injury compensation packages, weapons, and amenities including cell-phones, and vehicles. A delegate expressed that the magnitude of the problem is best understood if we consider the plight of the 2 million unemployed males in FATA between the ages of 20 and 40. "If only 2 percent of that 2 million were to be coerced into militancy, this would mean 40,000 new militants, which could have disastrous effects."[41]

---

41. Delegate comment during visit to Washington, DC in April, 2010.

THE MILITANTS' CAMPAIGN AGAINST TRADITIONAL ISLAM

Beginning in about 2002 until today, the core infrastructure of the ASJ community has been attacked and their members brutally targeted by the radical DW networks who are trying to dramatically alter the character and demographics of the Pakistan state. Numerous ASJ cultural landmarks and shrines of traditional saints have been destroyed including the mausoleum of a legendary 17th century Sufi poet known as Rahman Baba[42] and the shrine of Sheikh Baba in Bara Sheikhaan in Landi Kotal. In Nowshera, the popular saint Bahadur Baba's shrine was attacked with rockets and finally burned to the ground. In numerous cases, bodies of saints and religious leaders have been disinterred and publically desecrated. Popular demonstrations often follow such attacks; after the Landi Kotal attack, 22 demonstrators were murdered by violent extremists.[43]

According to a leading ASJ educator from Multan, ASJ mosques and schools, some of which were founded before the creation of Pakistan, are being taken over by extremists through the force of weapons. Quite often ASJ signs and slogans on mosques are defaced and replaced with extremist ideological slogans.[44]

Despite DW efforts to *"Talibanize"* Pakistan's tribal frontier, grassroots communities in this region are resisting the hostile takeover of their social structure and hundreds have died to prevent it. According to local sources, in North and South Waziristan alone, thousands of religious leaders and over 1000 elders and tribal *maliks* who partook in tribal *jirgas* have been assassinated by insurgents since 2002.[45] Religious and political leaders in conflict areas report that they and their families receive death threats daily through phone calls and SMS texts.

---

42. "Attack on Rehman Baba is Attack on Pashtun Identity," *Daily Times*, March 07, 2009, http://www.dailytimes.com.pk/default.asp?page=2009%5C03%5C07%5Cstory_7-3-2009_pg3_1 (accessed April 15, 2010).
43. Delegate comments during recent visit to Washington DC in April, 2010.
44. Ibid.
45. Ibid.

The following examples of recent brutal attacks on traditional religious leaders throughout Pakistan were presented by delegation members:

- In January, 2009 in Peshawar the Sufi scholar and spiritual leader Hafiz Rafiullah was kidnapped and brutally decapitated.
- In Swat, the ASJ leader Mawlana Khan Bahadur was murdered in front of his wife and daughter, and his body was tied and dragged behind a car throughout the area.
- In June 2009, a suicide bomber killed Sarfraz Naeemi, a popular religious leader who openly spoke against the Taliban and sectarian violence in his madrasa.[46]
- Federal Minister and ASJ leader Pir Nur-ul-Haq Qadri who has been leading the anti-Taliban movement from his native Khyber Agency in FATA, has been targeted on multiple instances. Six of his close family members were recently assassinated, and 16 family members kidnapped.[47]
- The Federal Minister for Religious Affairs of Pakistan, Hamid Saeed Qazmi, who has spoken out publically about Sufi Islam as "the true Islam of Pakistan"[48] was targeted in an attack in September, 2009 in Islamabad. His driver and bodyguard were killed and Minister Qazmi has undergone three operations.[49]

---

46. "Bomb Kills Senior Pakistan Cleric," *BBC News*, June 12, 2009, http://news.bbc.co.uk/2/hi/south_asia/8096776.stm, (accessed May 18, 2010).
47. "Ulema, Mushaikh Declare Suicide Attacks Un-Islamic," *Dawn*, December 19, 2009, http://www.dawn.com/wps/wcm/connect/dawn-content-library/dawn/news/pakistan/06-ulema-mushaikh-declare-suicide-attacks-un-islamic-rs-05 (accessed May 18, 2010).
48. Delegate comments during recent visit to Washington DC in April, 2010.
49. Munawer Azeem, "Audacious Attack on Minister in Capital; Driver Killed," *Dawn*, September 3, 2009, http://www.dawn.com/wps/wcm/connect/dawn-content-library/dawn/news/pakistan/04-gunmen-wound-pakistan-religious-affairs-minister-qs-10 (accessed May 18, 2010).

PUBLIC OPINION IN PAKISTAN

INITIALLY PUBLIC OPINION AND THE MEDIA IN PAKISTAN did not perceive the Pakistani Taliban and affiliated radical DW factions as an existential and immediate threat. What were once perceived as a localized "band of thugs," eventually became a large menace, spreading violence throughout the frontier and Punjab. It was not until people personally witnessed the Taliban's brutality, immorality, and self-serving criminality, that the tide was turned against them.[50] Whatever leverage that was gained by capitalizing on the public dissatisfaction with the US war in Afghanistan and on painting themselves as purveyors of authentic Islam and providers of social justice – has been lost as a result of the suicide attacks that have ripped through Pakistan.

A delegate pointed out that after major attacks, such as the blast which killed over 100 people at a Meena Bazaar[51] in Peshawar (a market primarily catering to women and children), the population in the frontier regions has been vocal about their opposition to the Taliban and the "unIslamic" nature of their activities.[52] Sermons of ASJ clerics and social activists, often delivered at great personal risk, have been critical to changing the public opinion.

After the successful Pakistani military operations in Swat and the Frontier, Pakistani's media and civil society increasingly assert that the tide is turning against extremists, and that the military's successes have emboldened more people to partake in anti-Taliban efforts.

---

50. Husain Haqqani, "How Pakistan is Countering the Taliban," *The Wall Street Journal*, April 30, 2009, http://online.wsj.com/article/SB124096805456666593.html (accessed April 15, 2010).
51. Ali Hazrat Bacha, "Death toll from Peshawar blast rises to 117," *Dawn*, October 30, 2009, http://www.dawn.com/wps/wcm/connect/dawn-content-library/dawn/news/pakistan/metropolitan/04-explosion-heard-peshawar-qs-04 (accessed April 15, 2010).
52. Delegate comment during visit to Washington, DC in April, 2010.

RECOMMENDATIONS

ASJ LEADERS ARE NATURALLY POSITIONED TO COUNTER radical ideologies but they need international support and recognition. Notwithstanding the disparate odds facing the ASJ, their various groups and leaders have come together to launch a campaign to save their districts from militants and to save Pakistan from disintegration. When the army launched offensives in Swat and Buner, it was the ASJ networks of leaders and clerics they turned to for support, knowing that they would influence grassroots public opinion in favor of military action.[53] ASJ are also actively engaged in building pressure on the Pakistan government to take concrete steps against the extremists.

WORKING WITH MODERATE LEADERS TO "HOLD AND BUILD"

As news reports surface that targeted killings have restarted in the Swat Valley, previously declared free of Talibanism, analysts everywhere ask themselves how can the government accomplish the COIN objectives to "hold and build" territory once military operations have "cleared" an area. The ASJ networks in Pakistan are particularly important for this purpose.

In their meetings with US policymakers, the delegates stressed that there are two distinct categories of extremists. The first are those violent militants who are motivated almost entirely by the radical DW ideology with inherently malignant designs, who seek to expand their base of power and oppress the general population. These extremists need to be treated with force, and military action against them is essential. Once that group is controlled or removed from the local population, the second group who participate largely out of a desire for economic and social advancement, coupled with a radical Islamist ideology, must be deradicalized and reintroduced into mainstream society if the COIN operation is to succeed.

---

53. Delegate comment during Washington DC visit April, 2010.

Participants in the second group are often unemployed, young adults who turn towards the extremists – not purely on ideological designs, but for economic benefits because the militants offer cash, vehicles, weapons, employment and education that the government and other private organizations cannot provide. There are two important components to "peeling" them away from extremism: a) providing a competing set of social, economic, and educational opportunities; and b) strengthening the indigenous moderate voice that can effectively counter and expose extremist ideologies.

For both aims, ASJ institutions and their leadership are the most ideally placed. On one hand, given their institutional capacity and legitimacy in even the most remote areas, ASJ social welfare organizations are amongst the most effective providers of social services, particularly in post-crisis zones. On the other hand, as religious leaders, the ASJ can best counter extremist interpretations and ideologies while providing an authentic, alternative religious paradigm that is palatable to local populations.

Forging Partnerships with ASJ Institutions

Despite the atrocities committed by the DW *jihadists*, previous analysts have failed to accurately recognize the link between the continuation of the conflict and the lack of support the ASJ receives from local and international players. Overlooked and underutilized as potential partners in countering radicalization and stabilizing the region, ASJ lack the resources necessary to compete with the well organized and well funded DW groups. When outnumbered and outgunned by the extremists, ASJ leaders either cede control of their social network or move out of the region. If they could be strengthened, they could curb the *Talibanization* of Pakistan. It is equally important to consider that working and engaging ASJ leaders and their institutions will also serve to improve the US image on the ground in Pakistan, since it will be construed by the masses as supporting the mainstream majority of the Pakistani people.

There are a number of distinct areas where we can explore opportunities to partner with and strengthen ASJ institutions to more effectively challenge extremist ideologies and provide social assistance to conflict-effected or sensitive areas.

- **Strategic campaigns to counter violent extremism:** The ASJ needs programming support for events, campaigns and conferences which speak out against terrorism and promote reconciliation and reintegration of the former militants back into mainstream society.

- **Education:** ASJ educational institutions need to expand their capacity to provide quality education. They need financial assistance to upscale existing institutions to provide secular education, vocational training, as well as religious and ethics education for the general population.

- **Social services:** The international donor community should strengthen ASJ social services organizations or create partnerships with these organizations to administer development assistance, humanitarian assistance for IDPs, earthquake victims, etc., or enlist their support to better understand local needs and identify credible partners on the ground.

- **Restoration of Pakistan's cultural heritage:** The preservation and restoration of Pakistan's cultural heritage including shrines, which are central to the traditional cultural and religious life of Pakistan, is vital to reinvigorating the voice of the moderate majority.

- **Strengthening the moderate voice through media:** The international donor community should provide technical assistance to ASJ institutions so they can learn how to maximize their effect in spreading the message of moderation and denouncing terrorism across Pakistan and internationally (e.g. communications training, media support, etc.).

Recommendations

It is important to recognize that the societal deconstruction of the tribal frontier of Pakistan has continued for over 30 years, ever since the DW groups were empowered to fight in Afghanistan against the USSR. As a result, many of the leading figures of the ASJ have either been killed or migrated out of parts of FATA and Khyber-Pakhtunkhwa; and, the people still remaining are either "hostage" to the extremists, or have surrendered to their ideological onslaught just to survive. This doesn't mean such areas cannot be returned to the mainstream Muslim community; but in many cases this would require a return of exiled figures and a redevelopment of destroyed cultural and social heritage.[54]

Across Pakistan more generally, it is also important to note that many of the ASJ institutions lack international standards of excellence because of financial limitations and a lack of exposure to proper training and capacity building. International donors should be advised of these limitations and should work to strengthen their core abilities because of their massive grassroots appeal and credibility.

---

54. Delegate comment during visit to Washington, DC in April, 2010.

THE IMPACT OF COURTING THE 'SOFT TALIBAN'

THERE IS AN ACTIVE DEBATE AMONGST EXPERTS in counter-radicalization and counter-ideology regarding who are the most legitimate interlocutors for mitigating the violence of extremist groups. In recent months, it has become quite popular for private aid organizations and US State Department officials to court allegedly "soft" DW groups in order to mitigate the violence and community support for the more violent Taliban factions of the DW. Though seemingly expedient in the short term, such support only further emboldens and empowers these groups in the long term to oppress the more moderate ASJ leaders and to demand imposition of their draconian interpretations of *shari'a* law in areas under their hegemony. In other words *temporary* physical security is gained – but at the cost of freedom of expression, women's rights and a future for Pakistan that is compatible with the modern free world.[55]

A prime example of the failure of negotiations with Taliban supporters of the DW was the attempted peace negotiation in Swat.[56] As one of the delegates explained, "The DW party in Swat (the Tehrik-e-Nifaze Shariat-e Muhammadi, or TNSM) started expanding their area of control after signing an agreement with the provincial government for the imposition of *shari'a* law. They behaved properly for only two days until the agreement was passed through Parliament. [After that] violence quickly returned and the peace agreement disintegrated. They took advantage of the truce to consolidate a Taliban presence in Swat; they advanced in Buner and took control of the holy shrine of Hazrat Peer Baba. Educational institutes were also demolished and civil government officers were compelled to go out of sight. Since then, a few more shrines were also bombed by these extremist elements. Many spiritual, (quiet and calm) people, traditional religious scholars and Sufi teachers were compelled to migrate to other provinces of Pakistan."

---

55. Hedieh Mirahmadi, "Picking and Choosing Enemies in Afghanistan," *The Huffington Post*, April 2009, http://www.huffingtonpost.com/hedieh-mirahmadi/picking-and-choosing-enem_b_190258.html (accessed May 3, 2010).
56. Zahid Hussain, "Pakistan Abandons Truce in Swat," *Wall Street Journal*, May 05, 2009, http://online.wsj.com/article/SB124144325468983215.html (accessed April 15, 2010).

The experience of the last five years has demonstrated that appeasing militants or hard-liners is at best a temporary fix, and simply does not pay off in the long term. A more effective counter-radicalization program is one that presents the recruits with an alternative religious paradigm rather than a mild form of the very dogma which was responsible for encouraging them into violence in the first place. Traditional ASJ Islam has increasingly proven to be the most effective alternative paradigm.

CONCLUSION

IT IS ESSENTIAL THAT US POLICYMAKERS learn the reality of what transpires in cities and villages across Pakistan not only to properly understand this particular country, but also because it is telling of the societal deconstruction happening across Muslim majority countries. We are witnessing numerous counter-insurgency operations not only in Afghanistan, Iraq and Pakistan, but in other countries such as Yemen, Somalia and even Thailand. The socio-political circumstances in each case are strikingly similar, and require common elements for success: forging partnerships with the traditional, cultural and religious networks that until now have been ignored as part of the solution. In order to realize long term sustainability in these various fronts against violent Islamist networks, we must empower the moderate religious and civic leaders to better protect their communities, provide social services to their populations and to theologically safeguard their youth from the dangerous allure of terrorism.